THE TAO OF CLEANING

THE TAO OF CLEANING

A. W. KU

Box Turtle Press
™

Box Turtle Press
William Penn Annex
P. O. Box 748
Philadelphia, PA 19105

ISBN# 0-9655743-0-X
Library of Congress Catalog Card Number 96-95133

Printed and bound in the United States of America

Grateful acknowledgement is made to Shambhala Publications
for permission to reprint quotes from
Tao Teh Ching by Lao Tzu
translated by John C. H. Wu. © 1961
by St. John's University Press, New York.
Reprinted by arrangement with
Shambhala Publications, Inc.
300 Massachusetts Avenue
Boston, MA 02115

Grateful acknowledgement is made to Tilden Press, Inc.
for permission to reprint excerpts from
<u>Products for the Ages</u>
from **The Green Business Letter**. ©1996 by Tilden Press, Inc.
1519 Connecticut Avenue NW
Washington, D.C. 20036
For subscription information or a sample copy visit their web page at
http://www.enn.com/gbl or call 800-955-GREEN or
email to gbl@enn.com.

Translations of Chinese to English in the <u>Appendix</u>
are from the following sources:

Read And Write Chinese by Rita Mei-Wah Choy
(Fifth Edition) © 1990 by Rita Choy Hirschberg
published by China West Books
P. O. Box 2804
San Francisco, California 94126

Understanding Chinese by Rita Mei-Wah Choy
© 1989 by Rita Choy Hirschberg
published by China West Books
P. O. Box 2804
San Francisco, California 94126

English-Chinese & Chinese-English Dictionary
published in 1965
by Da Kwan Publishing Company, HongKong

Translations of Chinese to English in the <u>Appendix</u>
are from the following sources:

Chinese Characters by Dr. L. Wieger, S.J.
translated into English by L. Davrout, S.J.
This edition,first published in 1965, is an unabridged and unaltered
republication of the second edition, published by the Catholic Mission
Press in 1927. The first edition of **Chinese Characters** was published
in 1915. This edition is a joint publication of Paragon Book Reprint
Corp. and Dover Publications, Inc.

ACKNOWLEDGMENTS

I am deeply grateful to Deng Ming-Dao for his helpful and encouraging comments about this book.

Special thanks to Alexander Ku who gave generously of his time and knowledge of book design.

I particularly wish to thank J. W. K. for his ideas, support and guidance in making and completing this book.

CONTENTS

Introduction
1

Housework
3

Hidden Time
29

Less Ado
59

Nitty Gritty
81

Sage Advice
101

Appendix
117

Housework

One step	(yi bu)	8
Learning to fly	(xue fei)	10
Impermanence	(liu sha)	12
Floating	(fu)	14
Simple doing	(su huo dong)	16
Follow through	(wan bei)	18
One becomes two	(yi bian er)	20
Keys	(yao shi)	22
First of all	(shou xian)	24
Foundation	(ji)	26

Hidden Time

Seeing anew	(xing)	34
Flexibility	(huan)	36
Cultivating peace	(he ping)	38
Keeping up	(bao quan)	40
Autopilot	(zi dong shu)	42
Lots of time	(kong xian)	44
Time bits	(qi)	46
Perseverance	(li zhi)	48
Yielding	(rong rang)	50
Opportunity	(cheng ji)	52
Trading times	(diao huan shi)	54
Know yourself	(shi zi ji)	56

Less Ado

Economy	(jie jian)	64
Giving is getting	(qi shi li)	66
Rotation	(zhuan)	68
Viewpoint	(jian jie)	70
An ideal model	(li xiang)	72
Variations	(shu fang)	74
Tradition	(chuan tong)	76
The right moment	(que qie fen)	78

Nitty Gritty

Flight plan	(yu bei)	86
Concentration	(ji zhong)	88
Fast Melting	(su rong hua)	90
Getting down	(ku gong)	92
Simple actions	(qi dian)	94
Possibilities	(ke neng)	96
Summary	(lue)	98

Sage Advice

Choices	(xuan ze)	106
Harmony	(tiao he)	108
Rationing	(zhi)	110
Balance	(heng)	112
Luxury and calm	(jing qi jia)	114

INTRODUCTION

The monetary compensation for housework is small compared to the benefits it produces. Avoided, even disdained, yet housework provides the essentials for a good life. In spite of economic limitations or physical impairment, a place, clean, shining, and tidy uplifts the spirit and offers hope and dignity. Meanwhile, shirking the basic duties of cleanliness and order will imperil the smallest household or the largest nation. Starting with a degraded environment and lowered self-esteem the resultant losses will continue to mount. Housekeeping at the most opportune time—before a spill becomes a stain—this is the way. Low is high. Simple is rich.

housework

*Heaviness is the root
of lightness.
Serenity is the master
of restlessness.*

Lao Tzu

ONE STEP

一步

Open the door to your dwelling and
discover that chaos rules the roost.
You feel overwhelmed.
Dust balls tumble around the floor.
Piles of dirty dishes and laundry wait to be done.
A cloud of fine particles chokes the air.
Cope with your inertia.
Start with one small or urgent task.
Straighten up just one drawer.
Set the momentum going.
Move on to the next task and then to the next.
Reclaim the entire place.
Courage!

LEARNING TO FLY

學飛

Housework is the bane of busy people.
Yet having a clean and tidy place
in which to live or work
lends grace and calm to daily routines.
Taking care of your physical surroundings first
means you won't have to cope with chaos
when you are busiest.
If emergencies arise, you will be ready.
An orderly place is the foundation of
managing a busy schedule.
Satisfy the claims of order
and be free.

IMPERMANENCE

流沙

Doing housework rewards you with instant results.
Ironing erases wrinkles.
Mopping and waxing produce
a clean and shining floor.
Dusting and vacuuming make
breathing possible without coughing.
Yet what has been cleaned and polished
will sooner than later become dingy again
requiring repeated rounds of effort.
The results of cleaning are immediate
but evanescent.
Therein lies the frustration.

FLOATING

浮

Mop a floor to the strains of music.
Clean the bathroom and ponder serious problems.
Dust a bookcase
and listen to a language tape on your *Walkman.*
Stretch your limbs and your mind.
Or accelerate your movements
and turn cleaning into exercise.
Or clean and meditate.
Scrub a sink and don't think of anything.
Skim along
and relax to the hum of the vacuum.
Let your mind float.

SIMPLE DOING

索活動

After a long day of sedentary activities
indulge in the pure simplicity of housework.
Change the sheets and do the laundry.
Empty the wastebaskets and tie up papers for recycling.
Wash the dishes
and clear the kitchen counter.
Straighten up the dining area.
Spread a fresh tablecloth
and set a pleasing table.
Prepare a tasty dinner.
Enjoy the essential
physical nature of housework.
It can free you from stress.

FOLLOW THROUGH

完備

Completing one task simultaneously produces another task.
After dinner wash the dishes and pots and pans.
Later put away the dried dishes and utensils,
and clear the kitchen counter of forgotten clutter.
You may either clean up after a task or during a task.
Put markers in opened books and magazines,
close and stack them.
Collect dirty laundry and do a wash.
Cleaning up is always part of the work.
Spend a few minutes each day tidying up.
Things haven't changed since you were a child—
pick up after yourself; leave your desk tidy,
and you'll be ready for the next activity.

ONE BECOMES TWO

一變二

Is it possible to clean and cook
while working or studying full-time?
Is it possible to maintain order
when events are in constant motion, even turmoil?
Take command of your schedule.
Don't attempt to do too much.
Allow breathing spaces.
Keep things simple.
Because you know there won't be time or energy later,
prepare things in advance.
Do the wash before you run out of clean clothes.
Assume dual roles—
be a parent to yourself.

KEYS

鑰匙

Is it necessary to be both neat and clean?
What about being neat but not clean,
or clean but not neat?
Is it necessary to be either,
or can we skip neatness and cleanliness?
Neatness extends the appearance of cleanliness,
and helps overcome
the chaos of a busy schedule.
Neatness sustains you
until you can find time to clean.
Yet order and good health rely
on cleanliness and personal hygiene.

FIRST OF ALL

首先

Always allow enough time for
personal hygiene and essential maintenance.
Use your time wisely.
Look ahead,
and judge whether a task done in the present
will create free time in the future.
The gain in time and convenience may be extensive.
Know when to discipline yourself
and get something done.
Use self discipline as a tool
to establish order in your life,
but know when to indulge yourself.

FOUNDATION

基

If you know in advance you will be involved
in a time consuming enterprise,
get your house in order first.
Before the project begins—vacuum the floors,
clean the bathroom and kitchen,
dust the furniture, and do the laundry.
Then enjoy doing your project
free from household concerns.
Launch any undertaking on the foundation
of order and cleanliness.
Reap the rewards of preparedness—
efficiency and peace of mind.

hidden time

In making a move,

know

how to choose

the right moment.

Lao Tzu

SEEING ANEW

醒

How do we find extra time
in a tight schedule?
Think of the day as the entire twenty-four hours
rather than morning, afternoon, and night.
Think of the week as the full seven days
rather than five weekdays and a two-day weekend.
Think of the weeks ahead in the month.
Consider the overview.
Will there be any lulls in the action?
Change your perspective.
Where is time that you have not used before?
Where is hidden time?

FLEXIBILITY

換

If you wish to save time,
and your income is ample,
hire household help and eat in a restaurant.
If your income is more limited,
hire help and take out food occasionally.
If your income is scant,
you will have to clean and cook.
If you wish to save time,
and conserve your money,
use time intensively and wisely.
Make a schedule
easy enough to follow or change.

CULTIVATING PEACE

和平

Acquit yourself of
household and personal responsibilities
sooner than later.
Best to do chores before time becomes scarce.
Doing housework regularly
protects against unforeseen emergencies.
Encountering the unexpected, you will find
order to be a balm against chaos.
Do tasks before they urgently need to be done,
or before they become great problems.
Don't be caught with just minutes
before company arrives unexpectedly
to clean your place.

KEEPING UP

保管

Manage your affairs smoothly.
Make phone calls and appointments in the day
when offices are open.
Look over bank statements in the evening
when you can sit and do something quiet.
Include some housework everyday as time permits,
a few short tasks on one day,
more time consuming jobs on another day.
Slip cleaning and cooking into the flow of activities.
Don't let tasks accumulate and
overwhelm you
either with anxiety or in actuality.

AUTOPILOT

自動術

You've created many routines
to help you through the day.
In the morning you turn on a getting-up routine
which propels you out of the house on time.
At night you turn on a going-to-bed routine
which calms you for sleep.
Develop a routine for housework
to get essential tasks done on a regular basis.
Providing time in your schedule
to get your cleaning and cooking done
will keep them from becoming overwhelming.
Turn on the housework routine.

LOTS OF TIME

空閒

A block of time can be as large as
a couple of hours or more,
or it can be as small as five minutes or less.
You might be able to get all housekeeping chores
done in fifteen to thirty minute blocks of time
dispersed through one day or over several days.
Large, small, or medium blocks of time
are all useable.
Tailor your task to fit the time available.
Match the task to your current energy level.
Break up heavy cleaning into separate time allotments,
or do it all at once—try it both ways.

TIME BITS

期

Use small disconnected blocks of time
over the course of the day
to do small unrelated tasks.
In a few minutes you can dust windowsills,
fold clean laundry, wash the bathroom counter,
bake muffins, prepare vegetables for salad—
the possibilities are endless.
In those odd moments, perhaps waiting
for someone to call or for water to boil,
do a small task.
Know when to work these little units of time,
but know when to relax and read a magazine.

PERSEVERANCE

立志

Use small disconnected blocks of time
to start and continue a larger job.
Clean out a closet, dust an apartment,
vacuum the entire place—or prepare dinner.
Set a goal.
Work on a large job discontinuously.
It will get done, later than sooner.
In a crowded schedule, it might be
the only way to get large jobs done.
You will be amazed how much you can do
just by chipping away at a project,
bit by bit.

YIELDING

容讓

Fatigue locks you out of your schedule.
You planned to study,
but find you are too tired to concentrate.
You can't spend this hour
the way you intended.
Nevertheless,
use it for something constructive,
but not as demanding of your total alertness.
Use the time for a quiet activity—iron or mend.
If possible give in to fatigue and go to bed.
Wake up early.
Study when you are more alert.

OPPORTUNITY

乘機

When you are tired after working a long day,
a simple task becomes an overwhelming one.
If possible, complete chores
when you have enough energy to do them.
This might be early in the morning
before going out for the day.
It might be after dinner when you don't have
to prepare for the next day's activities.
It might be at dinnertime
because you have had a heavy lunch
and don't need a meal at the regular time.
Sometimes a small change
may provide a time and a way.

TRADING TIMES

調換時

If you have been trying
to get a million things done after dinner
when you would rather be relaxing,
you could try flipping your schedule.
Get up early and do a million things
before the regular day begins.
You could go to bed earlier, at 10 p.m.,
and get up earlier, at 5 a.m.,
and use the two hours, 5 to 7 a.m.,
to catch up on those chores
you are too tired to do at night after dinner.
You will enjoy seeing the sunrise.

KNOW YOURSELF

識自己

Get a really loud alarm clock
or two (or three)
so that you really will get up as early
as you intended,
and accomplish what you planned to do.
If you practice getting up early,
after awhile, you'll automatically
rise at an early hour.
You can get a lot done on a quiet morning.
If you are a confirmed night owl,
a regular one-night cleaning blitz,
every two weeks or so,
might be the solution.

LESS ADO

Practice non-ado,

and

everything

will be in order.

Lao Tzu

ECONOMY

節儉

Keep things simple.
Avoid clutter.
Be content with enough.
Consider upkeep
before you select your furnishings.
Is this something I can easily maintain myself?
or will this item require expensive custom care?
Stop accumulating things
before you are unable to maintain and store them.
If you wish to accumulate things,
plan for their care,
and use or display them well.

GIVING IS GETTING

棄是利

Recycle containers and newspapers regularly.
Cull out the clothes you haven't worn in years.
Donate these clothes to the thriftshop.
Someone may want to wear them.
Donate outgrown books and furnishings.
Give away things you are just keeping around,
and don't particularly like.
Someone else may treasure them.
Share things you don't need.
While the bargain shop will benefit
from your contributions,
you will gain valuable space.

ROTATION

轉

Do essential housework on a regular basis,
and add a different new task each time.
This way tasks requiring infrequent attention
will get completed with your regular routine.
Rotate them as needed into your regular duties.
Lack of time?
Drop a regular task from the routine,
and substitute one that must get done immediately.
Keep basic tasks few and simple.
Decide which you consider necessary.
Focus on priorities, but try to allow enough time to include
at least one odd job in each regular session.

VIEWPOINT

見解

Don't let heavy duty housework dismay you.
Turn changing the sheets,
cleaning the kitchen, defrosting the refrigerator,
scrubbing the lavatory,
vacuuming and mopping the floors,
into routines done at regular intervals
you set to suit your schedule.
Assigning time for chores is
the first step to accomplishing them.
Dedicated time for a large job
removes the friction from the procedure.
You'll just do it.

AN IDEAL MODEL

理想

Ask yourself what has to be cleaned every day,
each week, each month, every six months?
Dishes should be washed after every meal.
If there is heavy traffic,
it pays to vacuum each week or every few days before
dust and lint develop into tumbleweeds.
Mop the kitchen floor once a week for spills.
Use a one-step wax on wood floors every six months.
This is a reasonable schedule,
yet it would be difficult to keep all the time.
Then ask yourself, what is the least I can do?
and still preserve
an acceptable level of cleanliness.

VARIATIONS

庶方

There are many ways to organize your work.
Do all the heavy work on the same day
because you have time and energy.
Do all the vacuuming on one day,
so you won't have to take out and put away
the same equipment a second and third day.
Save all the lighter tasks for another day.
Sometimes, quickly clean each room in turn.
Another time be more thorough.
Do both the heavy and light work, and
rearrange and fix all the things in a single room.
Do the next room the same thorough way another time.
Changing will make the work new and interesting.

TRADITION

樸統

Spring and fall are the traditional times
for major household cleaning and renovation.
During these seasons temperatures are usually moderate.
Neither does cold prevent you from
opening windows for ventilation,
nor does heat sap your energy.
Take advantage of spring and fall holidays
from school or work.
Reserve some time then
for major housework and repairs,
or for unusually difficult tasks
you don't have time for the rest of the year.
Or make your own tradition for renewal.

THE RIGHT MOMENT

確切分

Wipe up spills on the stove or in the refrigerator
before they harden and require effortful removal.
Make it second nature to attend promptly
to things that require immediate attention.
Nip problems in the bud.
For convenience clean or defrost the refrigerator
when it's nearly empty, not when it's full of food.
In the autumn wax the floors and prepare a sunny room
before potted plants must be moved indoors from the cold.
Air out a room on a warm winter afternoon
before the heat has to be turned on.
Select the expedient moment.
Everything will be easier.

NITTY GRITTY

The greatest
straightness
looks
like crookedness.

Lao Tzu

FLIGHT PLAN

預備

Adequate preparation will speed your work.
Clear the way before tackling big chores.
Even using a one-step wax on wood floors
doesn't make this a small job.
Vacuum all floors.
(This can be done a day earlier.)
Move all light furniture off wood floors.
Put all clothing and newspapers away.
Empty wastebaskets and set them on a table.
Remove anything that would get in your way.
Help yourself cut right to the action.
You won't have to stop and go.
Now wax those floors in one fell swoop.

CONCENTRATION

集中

Assemble all equipment in advance.
Use appropriate equipment and proper method.
To clean a shower stall, get right in it.
Wash the walls with a sponge
and a non-toxic or biodegradable cleanser.
Provide a pail of fresh water to rinse the sponge.
Scrub the shower floor with a brush and cleanser.
Use a plastic non-scratch pad
on awkward areas and areas with soap buildup.
Dab mildewed areas with specialized detergent.
Rinse all.
To avoid a lethal mix don't combine your cleansers,
but realize different areas need different treatment.

FAST MELTING

速融化

Disconnect the refrigerator before defrosting.
Set four pots of water to boil.
Clear the refrigerator, and spread newspaper on the floor.
Provide a plastic bag to receive wet newspaper.
After the water has boiled set the pots
in the freezer compartment of the refrigerator.
The ice will start to melt immediately.
Sponge up the water and wring it out in the sink.
Replace cooling water in the pots
with freshly boiled water.
Be careful.
While the ice melts drain and clean the refrigerator.
A messy job done in record time.

GETTING DOWN

苦工

People have different levels of tolerance
for dust and grime in different areas
of their surroundings,
but everyone appreciates it
if the toilet brush is used immediately
whenever necessary,
or if spilled urine or blood is wiped up right away.
Maintain the toilet daily,
but give it a thorough cleaning
at least twice a month or more often as needed,
when you scrub the shower and tub,
and mop the bathroom floor.
Confront the nitty gritty.

SIMPLE ACTIONS

起點

When you first come home from outside
wash your hands.
This often means putting down bags of groceries
and going to the kitchen sink.
Keep the kitchen sink cleared for constant use.
Don't leave the dishes piled in it.
When you are ready to fix a meal or a snack,
first wash your hands.
If you are going to use it for food preparation,
wash the sink.
Simple hygiene
will save you from many illnesses.

POSSIBILITIES

可能

Early in the morning boil up some noodles.
Drain them in a colander.
Cover the colander with a plate and set it aside.
Returning home in the afternoon from a farmers' market
with leafy green vegetables,
rinse and put them in a pot.
Drain away excess water. Allow residual water to remain.
Add spices. Toss gently.
Cover the pot and keep it in a cool place.
In the evening prepare a favorite sauce.
Steam the cleaned vegetables using just the residual water.
Heat and serve the sauce over the pasta.
Prepare dinner before hunger strikes.

SUMMARY

略

Work smoothly without effort.
Dress in comfortable work clothes and shoes.
Wear waterproof gloves to protect your hands.
Select appropriate equipment and mild cleansers.
Read labels and use products correctly.
Maintain appliances
and store cleaning supplies properly.
Have all equipment together before cleaning.
Prepare the area before doing the task.
Allow enough time.
As circumstances change, adjust your schedule.
Tackle difficult things early
when they are still easy.

SAGE ADVICE

Here is the way of heaven
when you have done
your work,
retire!

Lao Tzu

CHOICES

選擇

A full-time job, school, children,
make consistency and a regular schedule difficult.
Cut corners, decide what is important to you.
Buy stainless flatware rather than silverware
and clothes that can be washed
and worn without ironing.
If details are important to you,
polish the silverware and press the clothing.
Cut back on something else.
Nothing has to be a certain way,
unless you want it to be that way.
Set your own priorities.
Create your own lifestyle.

HARMONY

調和

With children in the household, expect disorder.
Teach them to enjoy clean and neat surroundings.
Ask them to help around the home.
Things will be a little ragged, but harmonious.
If all members sharing a household
have similar standards of cleanliness and tidiness,
and are participating as much as they are able
in its upkeep, tensions will diminish.
Find a partner with similar levels
of tolerance for dirt and messiness—
someone who does not avoid work.
Happy is the household
where each does more than his own share.

RATIONING

制

To save time to do research a scientist bought
31 sets of the same shirt, trousers, and socks
to wear each day between monthly washes.
An artist prepared the same meals daily for herself
to save time to paint.
Another artist never cleaned his house,
but moved whenever the mess became impossible.
Still he felt there was not enough time to work.
We all pare down certain activities to make time
for the things we care deeply about,
but let moderation be a guide.
Weigh the consequences of longterm restrictions.
Make a conscious and informed decision.

BALANCE

衡

It is always a problem to balance the time
you must spend on the practical demands of living,
and the time you wish to spend on your true interests.
Pass over busywork, but give adequate attention
to mundane tasks that are essential
to sustain a healthy environment.
When driven by a single overriding passion,
still it would be beneficial to try for some balance.
Focus on your main concerns, but remember
taking time away from your central interests
may enrich your understanding and practice of them.
It is good to engage in both
the sublime and the pedestrian.

LUXURY AND CALM

静齊家

It is a pleasure to return to an orderly household.
Either you spend time maintaining a home yourself,
or you pay someone to do it for you.
There was an artist who said that her home
in addition to her sculpture was a work of art.
Certainly a household is what you make it.
It is an expression of yourself.
Because it may demand more time and energy
than you have, decide how much you want to do.
A clean and tidy household is ephemeral.
To have a consistently well-kept home is a necessity
as well as a luxury.

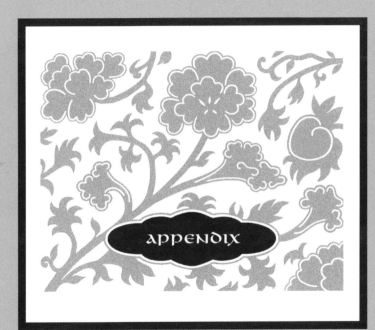

appendix

GREEN CLEANERS

Look in health food stores and mail-order catalogs for environmentally friendly cleaners. You can also find several "relatively pure and simple products" in your local supermarket. Some of these cleaners, well known and effective, have been around for a long time. They are mentioned in an article for Tilden Press Inc. entitled **Products for the ages**:

Arm & Hammer Baking Soda

Bon Ami Polishing Cleanser

Dr. Bronner's Pure Castile Soap

Fels Naptha

Ivory Soap

20 Mule Team Borax

Refer to the <u>Permissions</u> page where to obtain a copy of the article from Tilden Press. See the following page for short quotes from the article describing these products.

Arm & Hammer Baking Soda
Some uses: *mild abrasive cleaner that absorbs odors, removes scuff marks from linoleum floors, rinses hairspray and shampoo buildup from brushes.*

Bon Ami Polishing Cleanser
Some uses: *mild abrasive cleaner used on porcelain and stainless steel fixtures, cookware, glass-top ranges, cultured marble, fiberglass and ceramic tile; also used to clean white shoes, luggage, boats, and swimming pools.*

Dr. Bronner's Pure Castile Soup
Some uses: *mild soap that can be used for shaving and shampooing to treating athletes foot and purifying water; also kills the odor of diapers.*

Fels Naptha
Some uses: *rugged bar soap that is a staple of some laundry rooms, helps deter the effects of poison ivy, used shredded and sprinkled around plants as an insect repellent.*

Ivory Soap
Some uses: *a soap that floats, one of mildest cleaners suitable for a wide range of applications.*

20 Mule Team Borax
Some uses: *mild abrasive used as a disinfectant and mold killer, for killing household odors, as a polish for stainless steel and as a toilet bowl cleaner.*

SYMBOLS

This it the yin/yang symbol, the essential coexistence
of opposites, surrounded by trigrams.

The circle for heaven (tian) and the square for earth (di)
represent the "whole world".

This is the character for Tao, the law or truth of the universe.

MORE SYMBOLS

Bat (fu). Fu is a homonym for the word that means good fortune (fu).

2 bats represent redoubled good fortune.

5 bats represent the 5 blessings: a long life, riches,
health, love of virtue, and a natural death.

TRANSLATION

Housework

One step	yi bu	one step
Learning to fly	xue fei	to study or learn to fly
Impermanence	liu sha	flowing sand
Floating	fu	to float, drift
Simple doing	su huo dong	pure or simple activities
Follow through	wan bei	to finish, complete, prepare
One becomes two	yi bian er	one transforms into two
Keys	yao shi	key
First of all	shou xian	foremost, first, before
Foundation	ji	foundation

Hidden Time

Seeing anew	xing	to waken, be aware
Flexibility	huan	to exchange, switch
Cultivating peace	he ping	peace
Keeping up	bao quan	to protect
Autopilot	zi dong shu	automatic skill, craft or art
Lots of time	kong xian	free time
Time bits	qi	a set time or period
Perseverance	li zhi	to form a resolution
Yielding	rong rang	to yield, to allow
Opportunity	cheng ji	to avail oneself of opportunity
Trading times	diao huan shi	to transfer, exchange time
Know yourself	shi zi ji	know yourself

TRANSLATION

Less Ado

Economy	jie jian	economy, to be frugal
Giving is getting	qi shi li	to discard is to profit
Rotation	zhuan	to rotate
Viewpoint	jian jie	point of view
An ideal model	li xiang	ideal
Variations	shu fang	a multitude of means, methods
Tradition	chuan tong	tradition
The right moment	que qie fen	precise minute

Nitty Gritty

Flight plan	yu bei	to prepare
Concentration	ji zhong	concentration
Fast Melting	su rong hua	quick melt
Getting down	ku gong	bitter work
Simple actions	qi dian	starting point
Possibilities	ke neng	possibility
Summary	lue	summary

Sage Advice

Choices	xuan ze	choices
Harmony	tiao he	harmony
Rationing	zhi	to regulate or ration
Balance	heng	a balance, to adjust
Luxury and calm	jing qi jia	quiet orderly home

TEXT DESCRIPTION

Housework

One Step – Page 9
Starting on the way to cleanliness and order.

Learning to fly – Page 11
Prepare for a demanding schedule.

Impermanence – Page 13
Why cleaning is frustrating.

Floating – Page 15
Suggestions for a cleaning mind-set.

Simple Doing – Page 17
The joy of cleaning.

Follow Through – Page 19
The cycle of starting and finishing a task.

One Becomes Two – Page 21.
When there is too much to do.

Housework (continued)

Keys – Page 23
Neatness and cleanliness.

First of all – Page 25
Setting aside time to take care of basic tasks.

Foundation – Page 27
Freeing yourself from chores when you are busiest.

Hidden Time

Seeing anew – Page 35
Look for free time in a crowded schedule.

Flexibility – Page 37
Time and money.

Cultivating Peace – Page 39
The importance of tackling small chores.

Keeping up – Page 41
Doing what is easiest.

Hidden Time (continued)

Autopilot – Page 43
Routines smooth the way.

Lots of Time – Page 45
Different amounts of time accomodate different tasks.

Time Bits – Page 47
Accomplish many things with small units of time.

Perseverance – Page 49
Finish a big job in spite of interruptions.

Yielding – Page 51
Too tired to work.

Opportunity – Page 53
Take advantage of a change in the routine.

Trading times – Page 55
Switch the routine to get something done.

Know Yourself – Page 57
Change your sleep schedule to fit your needs.

Less Ado

Economy – Page 65
Knowing when you have enough.

Giving is getting – Page 67
The benefit of giving things away.

Rotation – Page 69
Getting infrequently done jobs into your regular routine.

Viewpoint – Page 71
The right approach conquers tough jobs.

An ideal model – Page 73
Draw up a list of priorities.

Variations – Page 75
Organize and reorganize your tasks.

Tradition – Page 77
Schedule your chores to be in harmony with the seasons.

The right moment – Page 79
Knowing when it is timely to accomplish something.

Nitty Gritty

Flight Plan – Page 87
Simplify tasks to get them done quickly—waxing a wood floor.

Concentration – Page 89
Analyze and tackle hard jobs directly—cleaning a shower stall.

Fast Melting – Page 91
A fast way to defrost an old refrigerator.

Getting Down – Page 93
The bathroom requires intensive care.

Simple actions – Page 95
Small precautions like washing your hands reap huge benefits.

Possibilities – Page 97
Preparing dinner in short bursts of activity during the day.

Summary – Page 99
Suggestions to ease your way.

Sage Advice

Choices – Page 107
Deciding what things make your life enjoyable.

Harmony – Page 109
Everyone can contribute to maintaining a household.

Rationing – Page 111
Devotion to your vocation may cause a loss of diversity in your life.

Balance – Page 113
Balance is difficult to sustain.

Luxury and calm – Page 115
The repose of a well-kept home belies the effort involved.

Visit our web site at:
www.tortellinibooks.com
or at:
www.boxturtlepress.com